# Boston Terriers

by Julie Murray

Abdo Kids Jumbo is an Imprint of Abdo Kids
abdobooks.com

**abdobooks.com**

Published by Abdo Kids, a division of ABDO, P.O. Box 398166, Minneapolis, Minnesota 55439.

Printed in the United States of America, North Mankato, Minnesota.

102025

012026

Photo Credits: Getty Images, Shutterstock, Thinkstock

Production Contributors: Teddy Borth, Jennie Forsberg, Grace Hansen
Design Contributors: Candice Keimig, Julia Line

Library of Congress Control Number: 2025936496

Publisher's Cataloging-in-Publication Data

Names: Murray, Julie, author.

Title: Boston terriers / by Julie Murray

Description: Minneapolis, Minnesota : Abdo Kids, 2026 | Series: Dogs | Includes online resources and index.

Identifiers: ISBN 9798384907503 (lib. bdg.) | ISBN 9798384908203 (ebook) | ISBN 9798384908555 (read-to-me ebook)

Subjects: LCSH: Boston terrier--Juvenile literature. | Pets--Juvenile literature. | Dogs--Juvenile literature. | Dogs--Behavior--Juvenile literature. | Animal behavior--Juvenile literature.

Classification: DDC 636.7--dc23

# Table of Contents

## Boston Terriers

Boston terriers are friendly dogs. Their coat markings look like a tuxedo. These **traits** earned them the title "The American Gentleman."

Tuxedo
Boston,
Massachusetts
N
W
E
S

Boston terriers were first **bred** in Boston, Massachusetts, around 1870. They are a cross between a bulldog and the **extinct** white English terrier.

Bulldog
White English
terrier

Boston terriers are small dogs. They can weigh up to 25 pounds (11.3 kg) and stand 17 inches (43.2 m) tall. Males are a bit larger than females.

Boston terriers have a smooth coat. They have white markings on their face, chest, and legs. The rest of their body is black, **brindle**, or seal in color.

Black and white
Seal and white

Boston terriers have a **sturdy** body. They have a short **muzzle** and large, wide-set eyes. Their ears stand straight up. They are often born with a **bobtail**.

Because of their short **muzzle**, Boston terriers can have breathing issues. They often snort and wheeze. They might also snore!

## Grooming

A Boston terrier's coat needs weekly brushing and an occasional bath. The **breed** can have crowded teeth, so regular teeth cleanings are important.

## Exercise

Boston terriers enjoy daily walks. They also like to play with toys. They are **sensitive** to temperatures too hot and too cold. They easily overheat. They might also need a jacket when it's cold.

## Personality

Boston terriers are happy dogs. They are playful, loving, and easy to train. They make great family pets!

## More Facts

- The American Kennel Club officially recognized the **breed** in 1893. Boston terriers are members of the Non-Sporting Group.

- Boston terriers became the state dog of Massachusetts in 1979.

- Gerald Ford and Warren G. Harding were United States presidents. They each had Boston terriers while living in the White House.

# Glossary

**bobtail** – a tail that is naturally short.

**bred** – developed over time for a certain purpose.

**breed** – a particular kind of dog.

**brindle** – having dark streaks or spots on a gray or brownish background.

**extinct** – no longer existing.

**muzzle** – the part of the head of some animals that contains the nose, jaws, and mouth.

**sensitive** – easily or strongly affected.

**sturdy** – strong, hardy, or solid.

**trait** – a characteristic or quality that makes a person or animal different from others.

# Index

Visit **abdokids.com** to access crafts, games, videos, and more!

Use Abdo Kids code

**DBK7503**

or scan this QR code!